Interview Tips: Transforming the Workforce, One Interview At a Time

L. Fentress

ISBN-13: 978-1530078899
ISBN-10: 153007889X

DEDICATION

There are so many people to acknowledge. I am grateful to God first and foremost for allowing me the opportunity to meet the wonderful people who have inspired me to write this book. From friends, family and the candidates I have had the privilege of interviewing or assisting in their career search. I thank you. I am looking forward to meeting new stories!

CONTENTS

What People Are Saying…

"When I learned that Laneshia was writing a book that would address interviewing tips, I was elated. As a human professional that I admire and trust, I know that this book will play a critical role in the successful employment of everyone who reads it. I would like to offer that sometimes the successful interview includes keeping your professionalism and cool especially when the interviewer gets off point or makes comments that inappropriate. It shouldn't reflect the company or kill the interview so always be prepared to control the interview narrative and only reveal what is critical to the job, the skills and the business at hand."
Crystal Brown-Tatum, Author & Motivational Speaker

"As a Human Resources expert with the gifts of communication, connectedness, and empathy, Laneshia sees the positive qualities in people that will allow them to excel, while desiring to help them overcome their weaknesses. Humor is often an effective medium for emphasizing what must be taken to heart. Laneshia blesses us with her positive humor as she weaves her true-life tales with her interview tips to entertain and educate both those seeking to hire and those longing to be hired. This will be a must-have for every prospective job applicant!"
Dr. Michelle Bengtson, PH.D. Neuro-Psychologist

"Laneshia Fentress has the respective gifts of discernment and encouragement. When she speaks, people listen. They not only listen, they learn. Whether you are in a season of transition between organizations, or whether you are in a season of promotion within your organization, it would be wise to listen and learn from Laneshia's writings. You will be blessed!"
Dr. Paul Vickers, Course Mentor

"Sometimes in life you have to just laugh and also learn vicariously, that is what this book is all about. Laneshia has a passion to help people better themselves but finds herself in some interesting situations along the way. I have loved hearing these stories and now cannot wait to read them all in one place."
Dr. Cassie Reid, PHD, Counselor

"Laneshia Fentress has the God-given ability to get to the heart of a matter and discern the motives of people from all walks of life. She brings a refreshing and uplifting attitude to the workplace as I have witnessed firsthand her professionalism, ethics, and encouragement to everyone around her. Laneshia possesses wisdom beyond her years from her vast experience with people from across the globe. Take this book and devour it as a master session with a human resources expert in hiring for Fortune 500 companies, but also a friend who cares about helping you transition into an excellent employee who will succeed in the workplace and in life."
Victoria Austin

"Laneshia has the incredible ability to captivate the minds and of her readers with a voice of compassionate authority which guides those seek the perfect job to the right position and eventually into their God-given purpose. This book will serve a timeless resource for the greatest assets in any company... People! Her heart so see people successful in life and in their profession as the driving force that will bring results the life of anyone who reads this book from hopeful employee to seeking CEO."
Dr. Brian Fentress, Music & Vocal Conductor

"Always insightful and charming, Fentress gives tips for interviewing in a manner that anyone can receive. We all know times are changing. Young job applicants seem to be unsure of how to navigate the world of applications, resumes, and interviews. By using humorous anecdotes and her own personal experiences, Fentress gives readers a compass to help point them in right direction."
Dr. Kimberly Gross Lake, Dentist

ACKNOWLEDGMENTS

I would like to take this space to express my gratitude towards the many people who encouraged me to write this book. I would like to thank my husband Darius for encouraging and supporting me through this process. I appreciate all of my family and friends, old and new… who saw potential in me and encouraged me to move forward. I could never list the names of the people who have influenced, encouraged and inspired me. Please know that if we have ever had a conversation about my vision, I think of you often. Your words have helped carry me to the finish line!

Introduction

Many people in today's society want the financial success and advantages landing a good job brings. A stable job not only instills confidence in a person's ability to accomplish a goal, but also allows them a chance to learn new skills that may benefit them in the future. Although finding a job in itself is an exhaustive task even for the most well educated, degree laden person. The task is even more daunting for someone who may not possess the same articulate responses to interview questions, or have the same access to resources as his or her counterparts.

Job seekers with criminal backgrounds, or those with language barriers may never be given the chance to prove their abilities. People re-entering or transitioning into the constantly evolving job market may also have a greater disadvantage than a fresh-faced college grad that received an above average education. Many times hiring managers make rash judgments towards qualified candidates based on their outward appearance, grammars or lack of experience. These attitudes only perpetuate the stigmatization of job seekers who may just need coaching or a second chance. The company may lose a potential star candidate with a unique skill set, and the job seeker loses confidence in his or her abilities to interact with people different from themselves.

In my experience as a Human Resources Professional, I have seen my share of disappointed job seekers who lacked the skills and resources to obtain the jobs they were applying for. The job seekers already had factors that precluded them from even getting their foot in the door. The job seekers then ended up spending more time and energy applying for more jobs without repairing the hindrances that were affecting them from obtaining the job in the beginning.

Because I have a heart for those who may be considered underprivileged in some ways, I have created a non-profit organization that will "empower people and equip job seekers for success in a field they feel passionate about." My organization addresses the unique needs of these disadvantaged job seekers by teaching them proper job etiquette, how to articulate responses to interview questions and how to find goals and a passion and transfer them into relatable jobs and careers. My empathetic nature and passionate desire to hire the forgotten job seekers in society will build confidence and change lives, regardless of the situation the person has encountered, the skills they may lack, and the first impressions they may make.

In addition to witnessing discriminatory practices of Human Resources professionals who ostracized job seekers based on appearance or lack of education, my father's work ethic has fueled my passion to help others find success and self-worth regardless of their current skill set. My father had big dreams of going into the NBA, but he put those dreams on hold when he learned he had a child on the way. At age 18, a friend referred my dad to General Motors and my dad has worked there for the past 40 years.

Although job security and financial reasons might have deterred a lesser man, these elements only encouraged my dad to stay with the company amidst layoffs, union issues and economic turmoil. To my father this was "his daughter's job," because it was a way to financially support me and the rest of our family. My dad also worked another full time job as a traveling musician while still working at General Motors to support his family. My father never let his circumstances, lack of a formal college education, or having a family to raise determine his success and drive. My dad's desire to master every new skill he learned and always giving 110% of himself is just one of the many reasons he was so successful at his job and life. His faithfulness to any job he received, and constantly seeking ways to succeed and being dependable, are just some of the important assets I believe job seekers today can benefit from. My dad did not let his current situation dictate his future success. If I can impart this wisdom and coach just one job seeker to adopt the same indestructible work ethic as I have, I can make any job seeker *shine* regardless of any external factors.

My organization will reach any job seekers who have the willingness to learn and transform themselves into stellar employees. One former candidate I interviewed even learned fluent English in a month after he was turned down from a job based on his lack of language skills. My numerous years of experience in Human Resources, and passion for helping job seekers who need encouragement, job training and skill development, make me a great resource to candidates of all backgrounds.

Everyone has a passion, regardless of his or her life experiences or disadvantages. My organization can make a difference in the lives of these future employees by creating transferable skills that can benefit any organization. When someone discovers their passion and receives the encouragement to set goals and learn new skills, they are no more disadvantaged than their competitors vying for the same job. We bring out the untapped potential in any job seeker and create an environment where the person will not only succeed, but will thrive.

1 ATTITUDE

Interview Tip #1

When you have an interview, the moment you arrive, you are being watched. It is always a great idea to be kind to the people who greet you at the front desk! Drop your bad attitude in the trash! YOU need the job, they already have one! #interviewtips

As a hiring manager, I have seen many good people with bad interview habits walk through my door. Interviews are perfect observation grounds for both the front desk staff and potential coworkers to study how you act in a professional office environment. From the moment you walk through the door of the building you are being judged by front desk personnel who are often considered the "face" of the organization. If you have a bad attitude, leave it at the door. Be kind to everyone you meet in your prospective next job. You never know who may have input in the hiring decisions being made. Interviews can be a nerve racking process, but being prepared both physically and mentally will ease the nerves and increase the chances of you leaving the interview with a job.

Successful candidates know that anyone they interact with once they step foot inside the building can be a steppingstone or roadblock towards being considered for a position. Candidates may only think to put their best foot forward when trying to impress hiring managers, but forget about the other people that are also important facets of the organization. There was one particular occasion where a candidate I interviewed was one step away from the hiring process, but disclosed to a lower level employee that he was wearing nail polish, a forbidden item on the company dress code. The lower level employee immediately reported his findings back to the hiring managers and his offer was immediately rescinded. Lower level employees, such as receptionists and front desk personnel, can be a liaison between hiring managers and other upper level management. Receptionists can be the first interactions between candidates, and their impressions hold more weight than some candidates may think in the hiring process. At a previous job, my employer had a system in place designed to weed out undesirable candidates. Transportation representatives would deliberately interact with the potential candidates to gauge their personality and stress level. The transportation representatives kept mental notes of their interactions with candidates and reported their findings back to the hiring managers. The candidates who were rude or had dismissive attitudes were not hired and were not even allowed to continue to the next step in the hiring process. I have interacted with many candidates who walked through the front door with negative attitudes and by the end of the interview process left with huge smiles on their faces. A candidate's negative attitude is just another side of the candidate's personality some hiring managers encounter upon first meetings. Although, many hiring managers may take a candidate's negative attitude as a snapshot of the candidate's work ethic, I saw the candidate as a normal person who may be going through daily stress and just happened to be applying for a position with my organization. Altering a candidate's negative attitude allowed me to not only represent my company in a positive manner, but also allowed me to get to know who candidates were on the most basic level. If the candidate continues to let their negative attitude invade the interview environment, then other issues need to be addressed. Candidates with persistent negative attitudes not only change the composition of the work environment, but are seen by hiring managers as stubborn and unteachable. Candidates need to be aware that any interaction between any employee and department can and will be monitored and reported, whether positive or negative. The minute a candidate walks through the door, his or her attitude, demeanor or bad habits will be on display for anyone in the organization to critique.

Imagine this scenerio...

Scene 1: Angry woman gets out of her car in the parking lot where a job fair is being held and threatens to slash the tires of the lady who took the parking spot she wanted.

Scene 2: Angry woman has to attend orientation class being taught by the woman she threatened in the parking lot.

Moral of the story:

Bonus Tip: You better treat people with respect, because you never know who you're dealing with! #interviewtips

2 GROOMING

Interview Tip #2

If you are going to a job interview, and you need a manicure, it is a good idea to take care of that BEFORE the interview, instead of picking and cleaning out your nails DURING the interview! #interviewtips

Imagine this scenario....

As I am sitting behind my desk interviewing a potential candidate for a position at the company, I notice the candidate picking and cleaning out his nails. It was really hard for me to not notice considering it was just the two of us in my office. Although this might be a nervous habit, you should be self-aware during times like these. Interviews are opportunities to show off your skills and impress the decision makers responsible for hiring you, not show them the buried treasure lurking underneath

your nails.

Interview Tip #3

Biting your fingernails, wiping your nose with your bare hands and playing with your hair is NOT professional behavior to display during an interview session. Try your best to leave your nervous habits in the car. #interviewtips

Candidates sometime wrestle with the idea of shaking the interviewer's hand and risk catching whatever germs are floating around the office, or foregoing the behavior and suppressing that physical contact with an unknown person. The influx of Germ-a-phobic people has made many feel unsure if the proper etiquette still exists for someone to hold out their hand for a greeting. Can you imagine watching the next interview candidate cleaning his nose with the very hand you're planning to shake?

Managers hiring candidates do not want to sit in front of Rapunzel or Goldilocks during an interview. One candidate I encountered had a nervous habit of twirling her hair around her fingers the entire time of the interview and never made eye contact while I was meeting with her. This nervous habit drew my eyes to the candidate's hands and hair rather than her responses or previous work experiences. Her nervous habits made me feel uncomfortable and negatively impacted the interview environment. Candidates should always be aware of their body language and facial expressions during interviews. Avoiding eye contact during an interview makes the candidate look shy, reserved, and introverted. The hiring manager does not have time to coax you out of your shell or wait until you feel comfortable enough to be present during the interview. Instead, the hiring manager will simply move on to the next candidate who exudes confidence and self-worth.

Interview Tip #4

Do whatever it takes to stay calm and confident during the process!

Usually candidates are given just one chance to impress the hiring managers enough to secure a job. Many times, even the most rehearsed speech becomes a jumbled mess of words due to a candidate nervousness. The most valuable advice I ever received came from my manager the day before an interview. As a candidate, I had the same pre-interview jitters most candidates experience on interview day. I was nervous and intimated because the position I interviewed for was with a well-known, established organization. My manager gave me a piece of advice about tackling nerves that I still rely on in uncomfortable, daunting situations. She told me that although potetential hiring managers for this position were interviewing me, I was also interviewing the organization to see if they possessed the qualifications I was looking for as the next company I work for. This piece of advice gave me the power to accept or reject the potential offer, position, and environment. These revelations altered my mindset and allowed me to look at future interviews not as a nerve-wracking nightmare, but as a learning process. I learned to respect the interview process and embrace the power I held to choose my future path I was given on each interview I attended.

Interview Tip #5

Do not let your current wardrobe hinder you from obtaining a professional job. If your clothes have holes in them and you do not own anything neat or professional to wear, visit your local thrift store or mission...If the iron is your arch rival, purchase a few outfits that are made with materials that do not require steam or heat. This will save you the hassle of spending time ironing clothes and whenever you are called for an interview, you can go wrinkle-free! #interviewtips

As a child, dressing for excellence was instilled in me at an early age. An entire generation of women ensured that a spirit of excellence and dressing for success were tenants of my core belief system. I remember vivid recollections of my babysitter buying the most beautiful dresses for me to wear. My babysitter not only ensured that I looked my best at all times, but even ensured perfect strangers looked their best. On several occasions she was known to stop young ladies in the mall to give them advice on the correct undergarments to wear with sheer dresses. My mom and my grandmother also took the time to custom make my clothes, and one of my aunts even created hair bows to go with my outfits. Every time my grandmother ventured outside of the house she made sure she looked her best. There were times I accompanied my grandmother on these outings to Penney's or Striping and Cox to purchase new outfits. Although at the time, these outings may not have been the most pleasurable experiences, in retrospect they molded me into the professional woman I have become today.

Many people in the younger generation do not know how to dress properly for job interviews, much less semi-formal outings. Some of these fashion missteps can be attributed to ignorance and a generational lack of concern for presenting a professional image. Although, dressing up may seem like a large inconvenience and gross waste of time to most people, it is perhaps one of the most beneficial deliberate acts a candidate can utilize. Potential employees and hiring managers may just run into their perfect candidate at the local supermarket, so it is wise to be prepared at all times.

Candidates should always be aware of their attire when preparing for an interview. Successful candidates will familiarize themselves with the organization's dress code prior to the interview. Hiring managers want to know that the potential employees they are interviewing and hiring will know how to act and dress in a professional environment. I have met candidates who did not read the company's website before choosing an outfit for the interview and have had to be sent home or risk the chance of having their interviews canceled. Men and women should practice good grooming and hygiene practices in order to be considered a formidable opponent compared to their competition. I remember one male candidate in particular showed up in flip-flops and socks to his first day of work. Many sandals and shoes can pose potential safety hazards in certain work environments and are unprofessional. Open toed shoes are also a prohibited item in most company dress code policies. Women should also avoid wearing open toed shoes such as flip-flops and sandals as well. Candidates should also avoid wearing gym attire such as leggings or tight pants when dressing for an interview. A good rule of thumb to follow when dressing for an interview is the outfit should be modest, professional, and not something that would be appropriate to wear in a casual, nonprofessional environment. Hiring managers should not be able to see any visible undergarments, tattoos, body piercings or panty lines. Candidates should be aware of what impression their clothes are giving to potential employers. Even though a candidate may have a stellar professional resume and know the right answers to the interview questions, if the candidate's attire does not support their overall professional image, then hiring managers may be receiving the wrong impressions.

Interview Tip #6

Some candidates may not be confident with making good hygienic decisions. One rule of hygiene is to always take a shower and freshen up before an interview. Bad body odor cannot be masked by strong perfumes, lotions or fruit scented creams. If you are unsure or not confident in this area, ask a friend if they have noticed any hygienic problems. You want to be aware of this before an interview.
#interviewtips

Candidates should be prepared to interact with hiring managers in close proximity during interviews. Successful candidates know and follow good hygienic practices including maintaining fresh breath and being aware of their body odor. Most offices have mints at the reception desk for candidates who may have hygienic concerns or want to ensure their breath smells fresh during an interview. Candidates do not need to ask for breath mints or disclose their hygienic concerns like one candidate who informed the receptionist why he needed so many breath mints. After hearing this candidate shout out that he thought his breath was not fresh, I could only hope that I would not have to interview this candidate with such poor manners. Breath mints should be taken discreetly from the bowl. Candidates do not need to announce their intentions or grab a handful of mints for future uses. Job interviews are professional places of business and successful candidates are able to conduct themselves well in these environments.

3 ETIQUETTE

Interview Tip #7

If you have an interview, do NOT take a group of friends with you. What happens if the person you bring, gets the job and you don't?! #interviewtips

Do you remember the old saying "Never take a friend with you to a job interview?" I have witnessed many candidates bringing friends and family to job interviews. Some people make it very obvious hoping to "score points for the team." Meaning, if one person gets the interview, they can inform the next person of my expectations. Some will go so far as mentioning their family and friends during the interview process. Some will try to hide it at first, but there are those you can discern if you pay close attention.

There was a mother and daughter who showed up for an interview one day. The daughter moved forward in the hiring process, but her mother was not chosen. The mother was not happy! How do you explain to a group of family members that one was chosen and the other was not? I had to be honest and explain to both of them that it is *never* a good idea to bring someone you know to an interview. If you have an interview, do *not* take a group of friends with you. What happens if your friend gets the job, and you don't? Chaos and jealousy might ensue.

Nervous habits equate to low confidence and employers want to know you believe in yourself as much as they want to believe you can perform the job adequately. If you do not have the confidence, pretend you do have it until you feel more confident in yourself and your abilities.

During an interview there is a large difference between self-confidence and arrogance. A candidate with an inflated ego will be viewed as a person that will not listen to instruction and be unadaptable in different environments and situations. A candidate should not have to list their every accomplishment during an interview. Instead, highlight one or two major accomplishments and expound on the details. Managers want to see the numerical and fiscal effects of your accomplishment on the organization. Candidates should be able to provide numbers, changes implemented due to their accomplishments, or how the organization benefited from those achievements. A hiring manager does not want to hear minute details of every great task you completed at previous places of employment; it will bore the manager conducting the interview and make you seem egotistical. Interviews are interactive discussions between the hiring manager and candidate not monologues. I have met many candidates who were so intent on speaking about themselves that it did not leave room for me to ask questions about previous work experiences or places of employment. One candidate spoke about himself so much I just had to stop talking and open the door. There was not enough room in that office space for me and his ego! Candidates should also be mindful of speaking while the interviewer is speaking and listening to the questions before answering. Good listening skills are vital to succeeding in a job interview. The hiring manager wants to know you will be able to benefit the organization fiscally and as a hardworking, teachable employee. A candidate should be able to sell themselves through their actions and accomplishments, not empty words and egotistical behavior.

Organizations state different rules and guidelines for employees and candidates based on the work environment and safety concerns. Some organizations are more permissive and lax with their rules, while other companies have more stringent protocols in place. Candidates should research the organization's guidelines and codes of conduct prior to attending interviews and orientations. A candidate's refusal to comply with the organization's guidelines may be hazardous to the organization itself and their employees. One particular incident I recall involved an employee smoking during a hiring orientation. The candidate tried to circumvent the current no smoking policy by smoking an e-cigarette. He pretended to chew on a pen, but was really trying to smoke discreetly. There is a clear reason for companies instituting no smoking policies. Smoking on company property can be disruptive to customers and employees and even hazardous in certain work environments. A candidate or employee who refuses to follow simple rules for a few minutes or hours cannot be trusted to adhere to protocol on a larger capacity or scale. Safety guidelines are created to protect employees, consumers and investors. Even though candidates or employees may not agree with or understand the current guidelines in place, they were created for a purpose. If the guidelines are ignored or dismissed by employees, there can be devastating consequences for the organization. Organizations can even be fined by government agencies if employees or candidates do not obey company protocol in adherence with local and state government laws. An organization that ensures the guidelines are followed correctly will be creating a safe work environment for its employees and consumers.

Hiring managers welcome job interviews because they allow a candidate to share personal glimpses into their lives as employees and people. Sometimes during interviews, however, candidates view job interviews as therapy sessions and divulge too much personal information. During an interview a candidate should be able to impress the hiring manager with their employment history, work ethic and personality, not scare them with their personal baggage. There was one memorable candidate who was so emotionally distraught during her job interview she could not stop shaking. I offered to let the candidate reschedule the interview when she calmed down, but she refused because she needed the job. The woman could not form a sentence let alone answer any interview questions. I decided to inquire about the incident that impacted the candidate so greatly. The candidate finally relented and confessed that she walked in on her boyfriend in the middle of an affair! Although the candidate was present physically, mentally and emotionally she was not prepared to attend a job interview. These extenuating personal circumstances of the candidate's life prevented her from focusing on the interview at hand and may even prevent her from completing tasks if hired by an organization. Candidates must be able to compartmentalize their issues and separate it from their professional lives. Although, I was relieved to be able to offer a non-judgmental, impersonal approach to the situation the candidate experienced, most hiring managers will not be so lenient when encountering candidates with issues not related to the interview. Candidates who are not ready to be emotionally present during an interview need to reschedule for a future date when they will perform at their peak, mentally and professionally.

A successful candidate will be knowledgeable and be able to follow proper professional etiquette guidelines. Generally, the same etiquette practices that should be observed in fine dining restaurants should also be observed in an office environment. Many fine dining restaurants as well as offices have certain dress code and behavior guidelines. Candidates should be relaxed prior to an interview, but not so relaxed that they disregard proper office etiquette. I encountered one candidate waiting in the lobby for his interview who had his feet propped up on the company coffee table. This behavior was unacceptable and embarrassing. Any behavior you choose to engage in while waiting for the interview to take place, or during the interview, will be observed by hiring managers and other office personnel. Candidates should be aware of the first impression and memories they are creating for hiring managers. Any negative first impressions a candidate leaves in the mind of hiring managers cannot be changed once the unprofessional characteristic is observed. A candidate should constantly regulate their attitudes, behavior and etiquette in professional settings. Unprofessional demeanors or attitudes or practices will be hard to stop once they become a habit.

4 WAITING IN THE LOBBY

Interview Tip #8

You do not want to be the candidate associated with the interview buddy with bad manners. #interviewtips

Your friends are a direct reflection and extension of you as a candidate and potential employee. One candidate did not receive the memo about letting friends and family tag along with him during his interview. His interview buddy decided to remove her flip-flops at the interview and propped her feet on lobby table while examining and pulling out split ends from her hair. Although she was not interviewing for the job herself, it was shocking to see her make herself so comfortable in a professional setting. Just in case you did not take my advice earlier about letting friends and family accompany you to a job interview. Remember this horror story.

Interview Tip #9

Save your selfies and photo ops for after the interview. It is not a good idea to take selfies while you're in the lobby waiting for your interview. #interviewtips

Although, as a society we are technologically advanced, there is still a time and a place for candidates to take pictures. Even though most people own some form of "I" something, taking pictures of yourself in the front lobby as you are waiting to be called does not look professional.

I'm in my office and I hear a man ask the lady at the front desk for a mint. He then says, "Because my breath really STINKS!" He was there trying to get a job. Allow me to suggest doing it this way -- just get a mint out of the bowl, open it, place it in your mouth and HAVE-A-SEAT, but keep in mind, the chairs inside of the office of a hiring manager are NOT for rest & relaxation! Fight the feelings of wanting to recline. Sit up straight, lean in and make eye contact! Oh, and no yawning and stretching during your interview.

5 BECOMING TOO FAMILAR

Interview Tip #10

While interviewing, I wouldn't suggest referring to the interviewer as "girl, girlfriend, or dude!" In my humble opinion, that is simply too familiar. #interviewtips

There have been many times that I would be in the middle of conducting an interview and the candidate would start a few responses with "Girlfriend, let me tell ya" or "Honey, I'll tell you anything you wanna know". I remember the day a lady walked into my office and she referred to me as "Girlfriend" a few times in our exchanges. I was a bit confused! I wasn't sure if she was just *that* comfortable with me, or if I was possibly giving off the wrong impression. Nevertheless, I remained professional and kind towards her. I get it. We live in the South, and terms of endearment are just a regular part of our language here. However, it is not appropriate to use this type of language in an interview.

In many parts of the world, people communicate their thoughts and feelings through animated hand gestures and facial expressions. Even though many people utilize hand gestures to relay messages, nonverbal communication can be misconstrued and may not be appropriate to use during an interview. One young lady who came into my office for a job interview used hand gestures to communicate a level of comfort that should not have been used in a professional setting. The candidate tried to get my attention during the interview and gestured to me with her hands from across the desk. The young lady remained unprofessional during the interview and did not refer to me as "Ma'am" or another appropriate title, but instead chose to call me "Girl" and "Girlfriend" during the interview. The woman's unprofessional attitude caused me to doubt her ability to conduct herself in a professional environment. Although I admired her ability to feel comfortable in such a stressful situation, an interview was neither the time nor place to forgo the professional attitude. Hiring managers notice even the smallest things such as non-verbal communication of candidates and their behavior in a professional environment. Candidates must constantly be aware of their demeanor, attitude and nonverbal cues before, during, and after job interviews. These sometimes-insignificant aspects can be the determining factor for candidates in today's fluctuating job market.

Interviews are not meant to be potential opportunities to meet your future mate. Interviews are conducted for candidates to discuss potential job opportunities, not potential romantic endeavors.

I remember one interview where a candidate was especially talkative and flirtatious. At the end of the interview he said," Man you sure are pretty!" After a moment of being caught off guard, I gained my composure and politely thanked the candidate. Apparently, the candidate took this cue as an opening to talk about himself and even told me how he picked out the sweater he was wearing to the interview just for me! Before he left, he made sure to ask if I was single or married. Not only did this situation make me uncomfortable, but also it made me want to finish the interview as soon as possible. Do not use a job interview as a chance to perfect your pick up lines or dating skills. Not only will you be out of a potential job, but you may leave with a restraining order against you as well! Show the hiring manager you are interested in the position and are serious about reaching your goals. Hiring managers want to hire ambitious candidates who know how to back up their words and examples with action.

6 PROFESSIONAL MINDSET

Interview Tip #11

When you are attending a career fair, it is amazing how much a smile can make you a standout. Consider your smile as a part of your professional image. A friendly face goes a long way! #interviewtips

I was part of an event where I had to interact with hundreds of people, and I noticed the majority of them would not smile. I started asking them, "Why are you not smiling?" Most of them responded with, "Because I don't like to smile!" I thought to myself, "How sad is that?" So, I started asking questions like, "Aren't you glad to be alive?" And "Do you have *anything* you could possibly be grateful for?" After asking each person these types of questions, I noticed they began to smile or chuckle. After breaking the ice, I would ask, "Why are you laughing? Do you think I'm funny looking?" The typical response was, "No ma'am, I don't really know why I'm laughing!" You can't walk around looking mean all day! It's impossible to do when you have an interaction with someone who cares. So I decided to start the smile challenge. No matter how intimidating someone may come across, I have made it my mission to break down that wall with the power of a smile!

Interview Tip #12

If you have an interview and you truly want the job, and you're not a morning person, I would advise you to get up and have a cup of coffee or something that will get you going. But take care of that before the interview. Never tell a recruiter, "I'm sorry (insert yawn here), but I'm not a morning person!"
#interviewtips

A candidate walks into my office balancing a large cup of coffee that is filled to the brim. My first thought was, "He didn't bring *me* any!" As we proceeded with the interview, he began to yawn and stretch. He then apologizes and says, "I'm sorry ma'am, but I am *not* a morning person!" I begin to ask him how he would handle a job that could possibly start out as an early morning shift. As he sips his coffee, he says, "Well, I would definitely need to think about that." I'm not sure this gentleman really wanted to work a job.

Body language is a crucial form of silent self-expression during interviews. Proper body language can be the difference between landing the job or being shown the door. Maintaining good posture and etiquette are essential during job interviews. There was a candidate who came into my office to interview for a position and behaved like she just rolled out of bed. The candidate yawned so wide I could see her tonsils. During the interview she continued to yawn and stretch as if she just rolled out of bed. Yawning and stretching during an interview is unprofessional and rude and makes you seem disinterested in the position. As a hiring manager, I never want to feel that I am interviewing Rip Van Winkle who just woke up from a 100-year slumber. A candidate should be alert, ask questions, and seem as if he or she is well rested. Slouching down in the seat not only shows a lack of confidence, but also shows the hiring manager you do not have the desire or energy to accomplish the basic functions of the job. Candidates' flaws, such as lack of sleep, or bad etiquette should never be on display to hiring managers. An organization wants to know that their time and effort spent on finding the right candidate is equal to the time and effort the candidate puts forth, not only during interviews, but after the candidate is hired as well.

Interview Tip #13

Leave all electronic devices in the car!

Cell phone use during interviews is completely off limits. I can understand if your phone accidentally goes off because you forgot to turn it off, but answering the phone in the middle of the interview is completely rude and unprofessional. If you answer your phone during the interview, you can kiss your chances of receiving a job offer goodbye. If you are expecting an emergency call during the interview and must answer your phone during the interview, immediately communicate this with the interviewer before you start the interview. Communication can be the deciding factor between receiving a job offer and having to continue on your job search. Although it may seem like many candidates would be wise enough to not answer their phone during an interview, there are some candidates who did not receive the memo. I have seen people not only answer their phones during an interview, but also respond to text messages. Do both the interviewer and yourself a favor by leaving the phone in the car.

Interview Tip #14

Do not contact the company multiple times demanding a status update of your application.

When you are a potential candidate, you must be mindful of the correspondence you send to potential employers. If you want to guarantee a special place on the national government's terror watch list, and terrorize a potential employer, send a threatening email. I spoke with a candidate once who could not accept my explanation of why the job he applied for was placed on hold. I explained to the eager candidate that I was still awaiting approval from my supervisor to re-open the position. Although, I was polite to the candidate after he called every day asking if the organization was hiring and when the position would be open, his constant persistence was bothersome. His continued contact with hiring managers wasted both his time and mine, and was not an appropriate way to show his interest in working for the organization. Even after he was given updates regarding the status of the job, he was still not satisfied with my response. When he ceased to get answers through telephone communication, he graduated to sending daily threatening emails. These tactics not only kept him from being considered a viable candidate, but it made me feel uncomfortable and fear for my safety. Although it is wise to keep constant communication with a potential employer to show the hiring manager that you are interested in the position, continued harassment of potential employers shows immaturity and lack of patience. The wait for candidates anticipating correspondence from a potential employer is never easy, but there are some ways the wait time can be used effectively. Employers welcome hand- written thank you notes from candidates. Everyone loves receiving mail, and letters in the mail are no exception. Candidates who write thank you notes show professional interest in the organization, and are also setting themselves apart from the majority of candidates who do not follow up after interviews. A candidate who makes a concerted effort to convey a professional image when communicating with hiring managers can separate themselves from other candidates who may not possess such a polished communication style.

Interview Tip #15

If you are more passionate about a job that is not closely related to the one you are interviewing for, do not allow that topic to dominate your interview discussions. Find what you are passionate about and PURSUE IT! #interviewtips

A candidate's job goals should be aligned with the position for which the candidate is applying. A candidate who has a passion for an entrepreneurial job should not be interviewing for a position where he or she does not have the relative amount of freedom needed to succeed. If you entertain the idea of interviewing for a temporary position, but only want a permanent job you will never be happy or successful. Following your passion is part of what sets you apart as a candidate. Unhappy employees will never try their best because they will always be looking for their next opportunity or the closest exit. I have interviewed people for certain positions who had lackluster enthusiasm about the position for which they were interviewing. But when I asked them about their passions or hobbies, their eyes lit up and they talked incessantly about their interests outside of the particular position. Although it is admirable to have passions and leisure activities outside of your professional job, it should never hinder you from being able to complete the job for which you were hired. Some candidates are so eager to receive the first job offered, that they do not look at the future consequences of accepting a job in a field or position that does not compliment their interests and strengths. Although, many candidates want the financial success obtaining a job brings, accepting a job simply for the sake of having a job is detrimental for the future success of the candidate. Candidates will eventually feel the stress of overcompensating for their weaknesses. And their lack of enthusiasm for the position will eventually take a mental toll on their mental health. An organization hiring less than enthused candidates also face several disadvantages when hiring candidates who do not have the adequate skills or interest level the job requires. The organization not only spends time and money training candidates for the position, but also incurs expenses investing in health insurance policies, retirement plans, and miscellaneous expenses. If candidates decided to pursue their true passions and career path and leave the company, time and financial resources are wasted. The company now has to invest new resources in advertising, hiring and training new candidates without the guarantee that the next candidate they hire will not use the position as a placeholder until their dream position opens. As a candidate, it is your responsibility to be honest with the hiring manager conducting the interview and let her know your intentions regarding the position and future career goals. Although it may cost you the position at the moment, you may have opened the door for the right candidate to be hired. Telling the truth during interviews may not be the most popular avenue to take when trying to impress hiring managers, but is beneficial in the long run and will leave a lasting impression with the hiring managers.

Interview Tip #16

Keep a good working relationship between you and your manager and, don't do drugs!

The hiring process consists of three variables most candidates will encounter when going through the hiring process. Most companies conduct drug screens, background checks, and reference checks. If the candidate cannot pass one or most of these screenings, chances are the likelihood of landing the position are pretty slim. Companies use drug screens to filter out candidates they feel may pose a threat to their organization either with safety concerns or the ability to carry out the functions of the job. Some positions dealing with machinery, or special equipment, or driving can especially prove hazardous to the candidate and others if these jobs are performed under the influence of narcotics.

Although some candidates swear by different methods to cheat the system, the best way to ensure a clean drug screen is to abstain from consuming drugs altogether. Once I overheard a candidate in the parking lot advising another candidate on ways he could pass his upcoming drug screen. The sharing of these frowned upon practices in such a public place is not advisable for several reasons. Law enforcement or even the hiring manager conducting the interview could have easily walked by and heard this conversation about drug use discussed so openly. If the candidate fails the drug screen, most likely they will not receive another chance to retake the test. A failed drug screen is one way to prove to the organization that you are not a viable candidate for the job. If you are applying for work, it is best to abstain from all drug use.

Many organizations conduct reference checks in addition to drug screens. Reference checks are designed to determine the reason the candidate left their former position with an organization and determine if they will be a satisfactory employee for future employers. Many candidates dismiss reference checks as unimportant and have the notion that most organizations do not bother fact checking a candidate's previous places of employment. While some organizations may not conduct reference checks, many other organizations will spend the time talking to the previous employers of candidates they are interested in hiring. Many candidates embellish previous positions and duties and job dates and do not disclose certain truths about why they left the organization or their duties while working for the company. If a candidate knows a previous employer will not speak highly of the person as an employee, or the working relationship ended badly, the candidate should simply omit this particular job as a reference. A candidate who may lie on something as small as a reference check is seen as untrustworthy, and is usually not moved forward in the hiring process. Organizations have more resources and ways to determine when a candidate is being untruthful than a candidate may assume. A candidate who is honest during the hiring process is a candidate who can be trusted on a larger scale. A job interview and reference check is just one way hiring managers decipher which candidates will uphold the moral attitudes and ethics of their organization. Even some candidates who may pass the drug screen and reference check portion of the hiring process may not pass the criminal background portion of the process due to previous misdeeds. Prior criminal records should never preclude candidates from applying for a position. Although some organizations may forgive the offense based on the date and nature of the offense, many companies will not.

Interview Tip #17

Just a little piece of advice: You do not want to make racial comments to a hiring manager during an interview! #interviewtips

Many professional work environments expect candidates to be politically correct and not offend potential employers or employees. Candidates should abstain from voicing their strong opinions on race, religion, and politics when in a professional environment. Candidates should remain neutral during job interviews and refrain from giving hiring managers their personal opinions on current political and racial events. One candidate I encountered during an interview was very abrasive and opinionated in regards to race. He felt comfortable enough with me as a hiring manager that he even allowed racial slurs and epithets to slip during the interview. His abrasive and offensive nature about race made me feel uncomfortable and made him seem like an intolerant bigot. Many organizations hire employees from various religious, cultural and racial backgrounds. Some companies in particular conduct cultural assessments that are created to see how candidates or employees perform in diverse work environments. Successful candidates are easily adaptable and comfortable in environments with a diverse population of people. Candidates who are intolerant of other races or cultures other than their own are a liability to the organization. An organization will only hire a candidate if they are confident the employee will work well with a constantly evolving employee pool. Many organizations conduct business transactions on a multi-national scale and interact with different populations throughout its life. Candidates who are seen as intolerable and bigoted can greatly impact the financial and professional future of the organization.

Interview Tip #18
Present yourself as a top brand.

Candidates should be confident when applying for a job. A candidate should never let their frustration or desperation be evident to hiring managers during an interview. A candidate will always maintain a professional demeanor and calm attitude when embarking upon their job search and interviews. The hiring manager should be eager to hire the candidate due to their skills and qualifications before another potential employer does. The candidate should always leave the impression that they are entertaining other job offers which makes the candidate more desirable to employers. Employers want to know they are hiring a well sought after candidate who can help their organization reach their goals. Employers do not want to hire candidates who are desperate for a job and will agree to anything in order to be gainfully employed. Hiring managers should be able to pursue and entice their desired candidate with their company offerings, benefits, and work environment. If a candidate is overly eager or desperate for a job, their attitude and work ethic will reflect this belief. Desperate candidates make rash decisions and can sometimes accept positions that will not reflect their professional strengths or financial expectations. I interviewed one candidate who was so desperate for a position with our company he begged me on his hands and knees for the position. Although I could understand his need for a job, his unprofessional approach put me in an uncomfortable position. A candidate should never allow the hiring manager to sense their urgency for the position. A successful candidate is aware of the unique skills and strengths they possess and can offer the organization. A candidate should never have to pursue or beg for a position with an organization. The right organization will recognize the attributes and benefits each candidate can offer the organization and respond accordingly. If a company is interested in a candidate, the organization will make an effort to follow up with the candidate and take the necessary steps to advance the candidate towards the next step in the hiring process.

Searching for a job is a multi-faceted process that involves intense preparation and research. In order for a candidate to remain one step ahead of their competition, they must be educated about the company culture and environment prior to the interview. A candidate must know the organizational goals of the company, as well as their strengths and weaknesses. Candidates should also familiarize themselves with the company's competition and financial standing. A successful candidate will know how their strengths as a candidate can benefit the organization financially and professionally. I have met many candidates who could not tell me which products or services my company offered consumers or even the position they applied for prior to the interview. The candidate's lack of research or preparation showed a lack of enthusiasm for the position and did not make me confident the organization could benefit from hiring this candidate as an employee. A well-prepared candidate shows the hiring manager that the person is dedicated, goal oriented and organized. A candidate should be cognizant of how their personal and professional goals coordinate with the goals of the organization. A candidate should not take the easiest route when searching for a job. Securing and investigating potential employers and positions involves hard work and research. A candidate should be able to determine the benefits and disadvantages each job and work environment can offer financially and professionally. Once a candidate has the pertinent information regarding each position and its expectations, the candidate can utilize this information to make a well-informed decision. The best decision will be advantageous to the organization and help the candidate reach his or her professional goals.

Interview Tip #19

Look at your past experience as training ground for your next opportunity.

There are many positions a candidate will hold during his or her life as an employee that will not be consistent with their organizational, financial or professional goals. Many students take positions to earn extra money while in school that are inconsistent with their future ambitions. Other reasons people may accept jobs they either don't like or want are due to financial constraints or lack of education or experience. Although a candidate may be working for an employer or organization that does not meet their professional needs at the time, the candidate can still gain new skills or experiences that may benefit them in the future. Candidates should not see their current job or financial situation as permanent, but rather as a stepping stone to aid them in their future endeavors. Employees should never let their unhappiness be visible to customers or hiring managers. Customers do not want to deal with disgruntled employees, and hiring managers do not want to employ candidates with negative attitudes. A candidate should maintain a positive demeanor when interacting with potential managers or potential fellow employees. Every position and work environment has the potential to increase a candidate's job skills and networking opportunities. A candidate should not let their current position or a negative attitude dictate their future success. Each position the candidate accepts has the potential to positively impact their professional career regardless of how menial the position may seem. A successful candidate will recognize the benefits each position offers and be able to extract the knowledge needed to be a competitor in today's fluctuating job market.

I recall many times, as I would interview candidates, I would ask questions about how they heard about the job or what attracted them most to the position. I can't tell you how many times I heard, "My wife filled out the application for me and the next thing I know, I'm getting a call to interview, so I didn't really have time to read up on the job."

Interview Tip #20

When you are looking for a new job or career path, keep in mind YOU are interviewing the company just as much as they are interviewing you! Be prepared with questions that show you're interested and serious about your goals.

I hope you are inspired by the message in this book. Ultimately, I want you to know that you can succeed at anything you put your heart, your mind and your hands to.

Made in the USA
San Bernardino, CA
10 April 2016